Ethics in Artificial Intelligence

A Complete Guide to Responsible AI

MERITE

Dedicated to my nerdy Son,
Shalom.

TABLE OF CONTENTS

Reference list

Appendixes

Artificial Intelligence (AI) is no longer the domain of science fiction; it has become a defining force in our world. From the smartphones in our hands to the algorithms shaping industries, AI is revolutionizing how we live, work, and interact. It holds immense potential to solve complex problems, improve efficiency, and unlock new possibilities. Yet, as with any powerful tool, AI comes with risks and challenges that demand careful consideration.

This book, *Ethics in Artificial Intelligence: A Guide to Responsible AI*, is a journey into the heart of AI's ethical dimensions. It is about understanding how this transformative technology works, the profound impact it has on individuals and society, and the principles needed to navigate its complexities responsibly.

Why Ethics in AI Matters

At its best, AI has the potential to enhance human well-being, address global challenges, and foster innovation. Imagine an AI system that detects cancer earlier than ever before, saving countless lives. Envision an educational platform that personalizes learning for every child, regardless of their location or background. Picture smart cities that optimize energy use and reduce waste, combating climate change.

Yet, these promises come with significant risks. AI systems can inherit and amplify biases, invade privacy, displace workers, and concentrate power in the hands of a few. For instance, facial recognition technology has been used to monitor citizens without consent, raising questions about individual freedoms. Predictive policing algorithms have perpetuated racial biases, and automation has left many workers uncertain about their future.

The dual nature of AI—as both a force for good and a potential source of harm—makes ethics an essential framework for its development

1

and deployment. The question is not just what AI can do, but what it *should* do.

What This Book Covers

This book provides a comprehensive exploration of the ethical challenges and opportunities in AI, structured to guide readers through its foundational principles, practical applications, and broader societal implications. Across the chapters, we delve into:

- **Understanding AI**: How it works, its history, and its transformative potential.
- **Core Ethical Principles**: Fairness, transparency, accountability, privacy, and safety.
- **Real-World Challenges**: Bias in algorithms, job displacement, and privacy concerns.
- **Industry Applications**: AI in healthcare, finance, education, and creative industries.
- **Global Perspectives**: The role of AI in development, democracy, and sustainability.

Each chapter combines accessible explanations, real-world examples, and actionable insights, making it valuable for both experts and non-experts. Whether you are an AI developer, a policymaker, or simply a curious reader, this book equips you with the knowledge to engage critically with AI and its ethical implications.

Who This Book Is For

This book is for anyone who wants to understand AI's ethical dimensions and how it is shaping the world. It is for:

- **Professionals**: Developers, business leaders, and educators seeking to align AI practices with ethical standards.
- **Policymakers and Advocates**: Those crafting regulations and guidelines to ensure AI serves the public good.

- **Students and Enthusiasts**: Anyone curious about AI's capabilities, challenges, and future.

By exploring ethical questions, this book aims to empower readers to become informed participants in the AI-driven future, ensuring that its benefits are shared and its risks minimized.

A Call to Action

AI is a reflection of the society that creates it. Its impact is not predetermined but shaped by the decisions we make today. Will we build AI systems that reinforce inequality or ones that uplift humanity? Will we prioritize profits over principles, or will we use this technology to address the world's most pressing challenges?

The answers to these questions lie in our collective actions. This book is a call to action—a guide for building a future where AI is a force for good, rooted in ethics and responsibility. Together, let's navigate the complexities of AI, harness its potential, and ensure that it serves humanity equitably and responsibly.

Welcome to the journey of exploring *Ethics in Artificial Intelligence: A Guide to Responsible AI*. Let's begin.

Chapter 1

What is Artificial Intelligence?

Artificial Intelligence (AI) is one of the most transformative technologies of our time, shaping the way we live, work, and interact with the world around us. From virtual assistants that help us schedule our day to algorithms that recommend what to watch on Netflix, AI has seamlessly integrated into our lives. Yet, many people have only a vague understanding of what AI truly is. To grasp its ethical implications, we must first understand its essence, history, and applications.

At its simplest, Artificial Intelligence refers to the simulation of human intelligence by machines. These machines are programmed to think, learn, and make decisions, often performing tasks that would typically require human intervention. Unlike traditional computer programs that follow fixed instructions, AI systems learn and adapt over time, improving their performance with every iteration. This adaptability is largely achieved through a process called **machine learning**, where AI systems are trained on vast amounts of data to recognize patterns and make predictions. For instance, when a photo app tags a friend in a picture, it's using AI to identify facial features based on prior data it has analyzed.

The Journey of AI: From Idea to Reality

AI's journey began long before it became a household term. In 1956, the concept of Artificial Intelligence was formally introduced during a conference at Dartmouth College. Researchers were optimistic about the potential of machines to replicate human intelligence, predicting that major breakthroughs were just around the corner. Early AI programs could perform tasks like solving mathematical problems, but their capabilities were limited by the technology of the time. Computers were slow, and data was scarce.

The enthusiasm for AI waned in the 1970s and 1980s during a period known as the "AI Winter." Funding dried up as progress stalled, and the grand promises of AI researchers seemed unfulfilled. However, the 1990s marked a turning point. With advances in computing power, the internet providing access to massive amounts of data, and new algorithms like neural networks, AI began to achieve remarkable feats. Today, AI powers everything from self-driving cars to personalized healthcare solutions, cementing its role as a cornerstone of modern technology.

Understanding the Types of AI

AI is not a one-size-fits-all technology. Instead, it encompasses a spectrum of capabilities that range from simple to highly complex. Most of the AI systems we interact with today fall under what is known as **Narrow AI**. These systems are designed to perform specific tasks, like recommending movies, filtering spam emails, or recognizing faces in photos. While Narrow AI excels at its designated tasks, it cannot function beyond them. For instance, an AI that identifies fraudulent credit card transactions cannot suddenly learn how to drive a car or write a book.

The idea of **General AI**, on the other hand, represents a machine that can perform any intellectual task a human can do. This level of AI remains theoretical, and while researchers are working toward it, it raises profound questions about control and ethics. Beyond General AI lies the concept of **Superintelligent AI**, a system that surpasses human intelligence in every domain, from scientific research to emotional understanding. While the idea of Superintelligent AI is often relegated to science fiction, its potential implications for humanity are both exciting and deeply unsettling.

AI in Everyday Life: Applications of AI Today

AI's impact is already profound, touching almost every industry and aspect of daily life. In healthcare, AI algorithms analyze medical images to detect diseases like cancer with remarkable accuracy, sometimes even outperforming human doctors. These systems are also used to predict patient outcomes and assist in drug discovery, accelerating medical research. Similarly, in finance, AI helps banks detect fraudulent transactions and provide personalized investment advice, reshaping how money is managed.

Transportation is another area transformed by AI. Self-driving cars, powered by AI, are being tested and, in some places, deployed, promising to reduce traffic accidents and improve efficiency. In entertainment, AI powers recommendation engines on platforms like Netflix and Spotify, curating content based on individual preferences. Even in customer service, AI chatbots are becoming the first point of contact for many businesses, offering instant support and resolving queries around the clock.

However, while these advancements highlight AI's potential, they also expose its limitations and challenges. For instance, self-driving cars still struggle in complex environments, and chatbots often fail to understand nuanced human emotions. These imperfections underscore the importance of human oversight and the need for ethical frameworks to guide AI's development.

Why Understanding AI Matters

AI is not just another technological tool; it is a powerful force that reflects the society creating it. Its potential to drive innovation is matched by its capacity to disrupt industries and lives. One of the most pressing concerns is the issue of bias. AI systems learn from data, and if that data is biased, the outcomes will be as well. For instance, facial recognition systems have been shown to misidentify people of certain ethnic backgrounds, leading to wrongful arrests and perpetuating societal inequalities. Such examples highlight the ethical responsibility of developers to ensure fairness and inclusivity in AI design.

Privacy is another critical concern. AI systems often rely on vast amounts of personal data to function effectively, raising questions about how that data is collected, stored, and used. While AI can improve convenience—like recommending a nearby restaurant—it can also invade privacy, tracking our movements, preferences, and even conversations. Striking the right balance between innovation and privacy is one of the biggest challenges in AI ethics.

Finally, AI's impact on jobs cannot be ignored. While it creates new opportunities, it also automates tasks, potentially displacing millions of workers. This dual effect of AI calls for proactive measures, such as reskilling workers and redefining job roles, to ensure that its benefits are shared equitably.

The Case for Ethical AI

One of the most telling examples of AI's ethical challenges is the use of facial recognition technology. In 2019, a study revealed that facial recognition systems misidentified people of color at significantly higher rates than white individuals. These errors led to wrongful arrests and highlighted the biases embedded in the training data. This case serves as a stark reminder that AI is only as good as the data it learns from, and biased data leads to biased outcomes. It also emphasizes the need for transparency, accountability, and rigorous testing in AI development.

Chapter 2

The Core Principles of AI Ethics

Artificial Intelligence (AI) holds immense potential to transform industries, solve complex problems, and improve our quality of life. However, its power also demands responsibility. As AI systems increasingly influence decisions in healthcare, finance, education, and beyond, it is essential to ensure that these technologies align with human values. This alignment is the cornerstone of **AI ethics**—a framework of principles designed to guide the development and deployment of AI in ways that are fair, safe, and accountable.

Why Ethics in AI Matters

The rapid adoption of AI has revealed its dual nature: it can be a force for good or a source of harm, depending on how it is designed and used. Consider a hiring algorithm used to screen job applications. On the surface, such a system promises efficiency and objectivity, but in practice, it may unintentionally discriminate if its training data is biased. For example, if historical hiring data reflects systemic biases—favoring one gender or race over others—the algorithm will learn to replicate those biases.

This raises a fundamental question: who is responsible when AI causes harm? Is it the developer who wrote the code, the company that implemented the system, or the society that allowed biased data to persist? The answer lies in creating ethical guidelines that hold all stakeholders accountable and ensure AI systems serve the greater good.

The Principles of AI Ethics

AI ethics is built upon a set of foundational principles. These principles serve as a moral compass, guiding developers, businesses, and policymakers in the responsible use of AI.

1. Fairness and Equity

At its core, fairness means ensuring that AI systems do not perpetuate or amplify societal inequalities. For instance, imagine an AI system designed to approve loans. If the system disproportionately rejects applications from minority groups due to biased training data, it can exacerbate existing disparities in financial access. Ensuring fairness requires both technical measures, such as auditing algorithms for bias, and societal efforts to address inequalities in the underlying data.

Equity extends fairness by recognizing that not everyone starts from the same place. It involves designing AI systems that consider the unique needs of diverse populations. For example, a healthcare AI system trained primarily on data from wealthy countries may fail to address the health challenges of developing nations. Equity requires inclusive datasets and a commitment to serving underrepresented groups.

2. Transparency

Transparency means making AI systems understandable and accessible to all stakeholders. This includes providing clear explanations of how an AI model works, what data it uses, and why it makes certain decisions. For instance, if a patient is denied coverage by an insurance company's AI system, they should be able to understand the reasoning behind that decision. Without transparency, AI risks becoming a "black box," where decisions are made in ways even developers struggle to explain.

Transparency also builds trust. When people understand how AI works, they are more likely to embrace its benefits and hold it accountable when things go wrong. Governments and organizations must prioritize openness, ensuring that AI systems are explainable and subject to independent oversight.

3. Accountability

Accountability ensures that those who design and deploy AI are held responsible for its outcomes. This principle is particularly critical in high-stakes applications like autonomous vehicles or predictive policing. For example, if a self-driving car causes an accident, there must be a clear process to determine responsibility—whether it lies with the manufacturer, the software developer, or the driver.

Building accountability into AI systems requires rigorous testing and validation before deployment. It also involves creating legal frameworks that define liability and establish mechanisms for redress. By holding developers and organizations accountable, we can mitigate the risks associated with AI and ensure that its benefits are distributed fairly.

4. Privacy

AI relies heavily on data, often collecting vast amounts of personal information to improve its accuracy and functionality. While this data can enable powerful applications, it also raises significant privacy concerns. Consider a smart home device that learns your habits to optimize energy usage. While convenient, such systems can also track sensitive information, such as when you are home or away, raising the risk of misuse.

Ethical AI development requires robust privacy protections. This includes minimizing data collection, anonymizing personal information, and giving users control over how their data is used. Privacy is not just a technical issue but a fundamental human right, and safeguarding it must be a priority for all AI systems.

5. Safety and Security

Safety and security are paramount in AI ethics, particularly as systems become more autonomous and integrated into critical infrastructure. An AI-powered drone, for instance, must be designed to avoid unintended harm, whether during military operations or in civilian settings. Similarly, cybersecurity is a growing concern, as AI systems can be vulnerable to hacking or manipulation.

Ensuring safety involves rigorous testing, continuous monitoring, and implementing fail-safes to prevent catastrophic outcomes. Security measures must also evolve to counter emerging threats, such as adversarial attacks, where malicious actors manipulate AI systems to behave unpredictably. By prioritizing safety and security, we can mitigate the risks associated with AI and build public confidence in its deployment.

Ethics in Action: A Case Study

To illustrate the importance of these principles, consider the case of COMPAS, an AI system used in the U.S. criminal justice system to predict the likelihood of reoffending. While COMPAS promised to make sentencing decisions more objective, a 2016 investigation revealed that it disproportionately labeled Black defendants as high risk compared to white defendants with similar profiles. The system's bias stemmed from historical data that reflected systemic racism, highlighting the ethical challenges of fairness and transparency.

In response, activists and researchers called for greater accountability and transparency in AI systems used in sensitive areas like criminal justice. This case underscores the importance of embedding ethical principles into AI design, particularly when the stakes involve human lives and freedoms.

As Artificial Intelligence (AI) becomes more integrated into our daily lives, its potential to solve problems and enhance efficiency is undeniable. However, this power comes with significant risks and challenges. Left unchecked, AI can perpetuate biases, invade privacy, displace jobs, and even pose security threats. Understanding these challenges is crucial for navigating the ethical complexities of AI and ensuring its responsible use.

Bias and Discrimination: A Reflection of Society in Algorithms

One of the most pressing risks in AI is the perpetuation of bias. AI systems learn from historical data, and if that data reflects societal inequalities, the algorithms will likely replicate those patterns. For instance, an AI system designed to screen job applicants might favor male candidates over female ones if the training data includes past hiring decisions that were biased against women.

The issue is not limited to employment. In the criminal justice system, algorithms like COMPAS, used to predict recidivism, have been shown to disproportionately label Black defendants as high risk compared to their white counterparts. This occurs because the training data reflects systemic racism, which the AI unwittingly learns and reinforces.

The challenge lies in identifying and mitigating these biases. While techniques like algorithm audits and fairness testing can help, addressing bias also requires a deeper societal commitment to equity. Developers must ask: Is the data representative? Are the outcomes fair? Without these questions, AI risks amplifying the very inequalities it seeks to overcome.

Privacy Concerns: The Cost of Data-Driven Intelligence

AI systems rely on vast amounts of data to function effectively, but this dependence often comes at the expense of privacy. From voice assistants like Alexa to personalized ads on social media, AI collects and analyzes personal information to tailor experiences. While convenient, this practice raises ethical questions about how much data is collected, who has access to it, and how it is used.

Consider facial recognition technology. While it can enhance security by identifying individuals in crowded spaces, it can also be misused for mass surveillance, infringing on privacy rights. In some countries, facial recognition has been deployed to monitor citizens' activities, sparking debates about the balance between safety and freedom.

To address these concerns, organizations must adopt privacy-first approaches. This includes anonymizing data, limiting collection to what is strictly necessary, and ensuring users have control over their information. Privacy is not just a technical issue; it is a fundamental human right that must be safeguarded in the age of AI.

Automation and Job Displacement: The Ethical Dilemma

AI's ability to automate tasks has revolutionized industries, from manufacturing to customer service. However, this efficiency comes with a cost: the displacement of workers. For example, self-checkout systems in supermarkets reduce the need for cashiers, while autonomous vehicles threaten the livelihoods of millions of truck drivers.

The ethical dilemma lies in balancing progress with compassion. While automation can free workers from repetitive tasks, it also creates economic uncertainty for those whose skills are no longer in demand. Governments, businesses, and educational institutions must collaborate to address this challenge. Reskilling programs, social safety nets, and policies that promote equitable job opportunities are essential for ensuring that AI benefits all members of society.

Safety and Security: Preventing Unintended Consequences

As AI systems become more autonomous, ensuring their safety and security is paramount. Imagine an AI-powered drone that delivers packages. While its primary function is harmless, a programming error or malicious hacking could turn it into a safety hazard. Similarly, self-driving cars must be designed to handle unpredictable scenarios, such as avoiding pedestrians in busy streets.

Another concern is the misuse of AI for malicious purposes. Deepfake technology, which creates realistic but fake images and videos, has been used to spread misinformation and manipulate public opinion. In cybersecurity, adversarial attacks can trick AI systems into making incorrect decisions, such as misclassifying a stop sign as a speed limit sign, with potentially dangerous consequences.

To mitigate these risks, developers must prioritize rigorous testing, implement fail-safes, and continuously monitor AI systems for vulnerabilities. Additionally, ethical guidelines and regulatory frameworks are needed to hold developers accountable for the safety of their creations.

Ethics in Action: Lessons from AI Failures

The risks of AI are not just theoretical; real-world examples highlight the consequences of neglecting ethical considerations. One infamous case is the deployment of Tay, a chatbot developed by Microsoft in 2016. Designed to learn from user interactions, Tay was quickly corrupted by internet trolls, who fed it hateful and offensive content. Within 24 hours, Tay began generating racist and misogynistic messages, forcing Microsoft to shut it down.

This failure underscores the importance of anticipating misuse and building safeguards into AI systems. It also highlights the ethical responsibility of developers to consider the broader social impact of their technologies.

Creating ethical Artificial Intelligence (AI) systems is both a technical and moral challenge. While the risks and challenges of AI are now widely recognized, addressing them requires a deliberate and proactive approach during the development process. Ethical AI development is not simply about avoiding harm; it is about building systems that contribute positively to society while aligning with human values. This chapter explores the practical steps and strategies for navigating ethical AI development, focusing on inclusivity, collaboration, and accountability.

Integrating Ethics into the AI Lifecycle

Developing AI systems involves several stages, from data collection and model training to deployment and ongoing monitoring. Each stage presents unique ethical considerations, making it essential to embed ethics throughout the lifecycle of an AI project.

At the outset, the choice of data is critical. AI systems are only as good as the data they learn from, so ensuring that datasets are representative and unbiased is a foundational step. For example, if an AI system is designed to assist in hiring, the training data should reflect diversity across gender, ethnicity, and socioeconomic backgrounds. Developers must critically evaluate their data sources, asking: Who is represented? Who is excluded? This awareness can prevent the unintentional reinforcement of harmful stereotypes.

During model design, transparency becomes paramount. Developers must document the decision-making processes behind their algorithms, explaining not only how they work but also why specific approaches were chosen. This transparency fosters trust and allows external stakeholders to scrutinize the system for potential flaws.

15

Deployment is another critical stage where ethical considerations come into play. Before releasing an AI system into the real world, rigorous testing is essential to ensure it performs reliably across different contexts and populations. This is especially important in high-stakes applications like healthcare or autonomous vehicles, where errors can have life-or-death consequences.

Finally, ethical AI development doesn't end with deployment. Continuous monitoring is necessary to identify and address unforeseen issues. For instance, if an AI system begins to exhibit biased behavior after deployment, developers must act swiftly to investigate and rectify the problem. This ongoing vigilance ensures that AI systems remain aligned with their ethical goals over time.

The Role of Collaboration

Ethical AI development cannot be achieved in isolation. It requires collaboration between a diverse group of stakeholders, including developers, businesses, policymakers, and affected communities. Each group brings unique perspectives and expertise, enriching the decision-making process and ensuring that ethical considerations are thoroughly addressed.

For example, policymakers play a crucial role in establishing regulations that set clear standards for AI ethics. These regulations might include requirements for transparency, data protection, and accountability, providing a legal framework that guides developers. Meanwhile, businesses must balance innovation with responsibility, prioritizing ethical considerations even when they conflict with short-term profits.

Community involvement is equally important. Engaging with the people who will be most affected by an AI system can uncover potential risks and unintended consequences that developers might overlook. For instance, if an AI system is designed to allocate public resources, consulting with underrepresented communities can help ensure that their needs are considered and met.

Tools and Techniques for Ethical AI

Advances in technology have also provided tools and techniques to support ethical AI development. For instance, fairness testing frameworks can help developers identify and mitigate biases in their algorithms. Tools like IBM's AI Fairness 360 or Google's What-If Tool enable developers to visualize how their models perform across different demographic groups, making it easier to spot disparities.

Another valuable approach is explainability, which involves designing AI systems that can provide clear and understandable reasons for their decisions. Explainable AI (XAI) tools allow users to trace an algorithm's decision-making process, making it easier to identify errors or biases. For example, a bank using AI to approve loans might employ XAI to ensure applicants understand why their loan was approved or denied.

In addition to technical tools, ethical guidelines and frameworks offer practical guidance for developers. Initiatives like the EU's Ethics Guidelines for Trustworthy AI or the IEEE's Ethically Aligned Design provide comprehensive roadmaps for integrating ethics into AI projects. These frameworks emphasize principles like transparency, accountability, and human oversight, helping developers navigate complex ethical dilemmas.

Building Ethical AI Teams

Developing ethical AI requires more than just technical expertise; it demands diverse and multidisciplinary teams. A team composed solely of engineers might excel at solving technical challenges but may lack the social and cultural awareness needed to address ethical issues effectively. By including ethicists, sociologists, legal experts, and representatives from affected communities, AI development teams can better anticipate and mitigate risks.

Diversity within teams is equally important. People from different backgrounds bring unique perspectives that can highlight potential biases or blind spots. For example, a diverse team working on a facial recognition system might be more likely to notice if the system performs poorly on certain demographic groups. This diversity not only improves the system's fairness but also enhances its overall quality and reliability.

Accountability and Governance

Ensuring accountability is a cornerstone of ethical AI development. Developers and organizations must take responsibility for the systems they create, including their intended and unintended consequences. This accountability extends beyond the technical team to include corporate leadership, policymakers, and even end users.

Governance structures, such as AI ethics boards or review committees, can help organizations maintain accountability. These bodies are tasked with overseeing AI projects, ensuring they comply with ethical standards, and providing guidance on complex issues. For instance, an AI ethics board might evaluate whether a proposed application aligns with the company's values or assess the risks associated with deploying a new technology.

Regulatory oversight also plays a critical role in promoting accountability. Governments and international organizations must establish clear rules and enforcement mechanisms to prevent unethical practices. For example, data protection laws like the General Data Protection Regulation (GDPR) in Europe set strict guidelines for how personal data can be collected and used, holding organizations accountable for violations.

A Case Study in Ethical AI Development

One notable example of ethical AI development comes from Google's approach to its medical AI project. In partnership with healthcare providers, Google developed an AI system to detect diabetic retinopathy, a leading cause of blindness. To ensure the system's fairness and reliability, the development team prioritized transparency and collaboration with medical professionals.

Before deploying the system, Google conducted extensive testing to evaluate its performance across different demographic groups. The team also engaged with patients and healthcare providers to understand their concerns and incorporate feedback. This collaborative approach not only improved the system's accuracy but also built trust among stakeholders, demonstrating the value of ethical AI practices.

Chapter 5

The Role of Regulation and Governance in Ethical AI

As Artificial Intelligence (AI) continues to evolve and integrate into critical aspects of society, the need for effective regulation and governance has become paramount. Without clear rules and oversight, AI systems can exacerbate inequalities, violate privacy, and even cause harm. Regulation and governance provide the framework for addressing these challenges, ensuring that AI is developed and used responsibly. In this chapter, we explore the current state of AI regulation, the challenges of creating effective policies, and the steps necessary to build a governance system that aligns with ethical principles.

Why Regulation is Necessary

AI operates in a complex and interconnected world where its applications have far-reaching consequences. Consider the use of AI in healthcare. An AI system that misdiagnoses a patient could lead to improper treatment or worse. Similarly, AI in law enforcement, such as predictive policing, has been criticized for reinforcing racial biases and infringing on civil liberties.

Regulation is essential to prevent these harms and ensure that AI systems operate in ways that benefit society. It provides clarity on what is acceptable and unacceptable, establishes accountability, and protects fundamental rights. Importantly, regulation also fosters trust by reassuring the public that AI systems are subject to oversight and not operating unchecked.

However, regulating AI is not without challenges. The technology evolves rapidly, often outpacing legislative efforts. Policymakers must strike a delicate balance between encouraging innovation and protecting societal values, a task that requires both flexibility and foresight.

The Current Landscape of AI Regulation

Globally, efforts to regulate AI are still in their infancy, but some notable initiatives are shaping the conversation.

The European Union (EU) has taken a leading role with its **Artificial Intelligence Act**, proposed in 2021. This legislation aims to classify AI systems based on their level of risk, from minimal to unacceptable. High-risk applications, such as those used in critical infrastructure or law enforcement, face stricter requirements for transparency, accountability, and fairness. The EU's approach emphasizes a risk-based framework, ensuring that oversight is proportionate to the potential harm.

In the United States, regulation has been more fragmented. While federal initiatives like the Algorithmic Accountability Act aim to promote transparency and fairness, much of the regulation occurs at the state level. For instance, Illinois has passed laws governing the use of AI in hiring processes, requiring companies to disclose when AI is used to evaluate job applicants.

China has adopted a more centralized and stringent approach, focusing on controlling the deployment of AI technologies like facial recognition and social scoring systems. However, these efforts have raised concerns about state surveillance and the suppression of individual freedoms.

These examples illustrate the diversity of approaches to AI regulation, reflecting differences in cultural values, political systems, and technological priorities. They also highlight the challenges of creating global standards for a technology that transcends borders.

Challenges in Regulating AI

Regulating AI is inherently complex due to its dynamic and multifaceted nature. One major challenge is the **lack of technical understanding among policymakers**. AI is a highly specialized field, and crafting effective policies requires a deep understanding of how the technology works, its potential applications, and its risks. Bridging the gap between technical expertise and policy-making is crucial for creating informed and effective regulations.

Another challenge is the **global nature of AI development**. AI systems are often developed, trained, and deployed across multiple countries, making it difficult to enforce regulations consistently. For example, a company operating in Europe may be subject to the EU's strict data protection laws, but its AI system might be trained on data collected in countries with less stringent rules. This discrepancy creates loopholes that undermine the effectiveness of regulation.

Additionally, there is the **risk of stifling innovation**. Overregulation can discourage experimentation and slow technological progress, particularly for smaller companies and startups that lack the resources to comply with complex requirements. Policymakers must carefully balance the need for oversight with the desire to foster innovation, ensuring that regulations are both effective and adaptable.

Principles for Effective AI Governance

To address these challenges, effective AI governance must be built on a foundation of clear principles that prioritize ethics and responsibility. These principles include:

1. **Accountability**: Developers and organizations must be held responsible for the outcomes of their AI systems. This includes implementing mechanisms to address harm, such as compensation for affected individuals and penalties for non-compliance.

2. **Transparency**: AI systems should be designed to explain their decisions in a way that is understandable to users. Transparency fosters trust and allows stakeholders to identify and address potential issues.

3. **Inclusivity**: Governance frameworks should involve diverse stakeholders, including underrepresented communities, to ensure that regulations reflect a wide range of perspectives and needs.

4. **Adaptability**: AI governance must evolve alongside technological advancements. Regular updates and reviews of regulatory frameworks are essential to address emerging challenges and opportunities.

The Role of International Collaboration

Given the global nature of AI, international collaboration is critical for creating consistent and effective governance. Organizations like the United Nations and the Organisation for Economic Co-operation and Development (OECD) have begun developing global guidelines for AI ethics. The OECD's **Principles on Artificial Intelligence**, adopted by over 40 countries, emphasize human-centered values, fairness, and accountability.

While these initiatives are promising, achieving global consensus is challenging. Differences in political systems, economic priorities, and cultural values can hinder agreement on key issues. For instance, debates over privacy often highlight the contrasting approaches of Europe and China, where the former prioritizes individual rights and the latter emphasizes state control.

Despite these challenges, international collaboration is essential for addressing cross-border issues like data sharing, cybersecurity, and the ethical deployment of AI. Establishing common standards can prevent regulatory fragmentation and ensure that AI serves humanity as a whole.

Case Study: The GDPR and AI

The EU's **General Data Protection Regulation (GDPR)**, introduced in 2018, provides a valuable example of how regulation can shape AI development. Although not specific to AI, the GDPR includes provisions that directly impact AI systems, such as the right to explanation. This gives individuals the ability to understand how automated decisions are made, promoting transparency and accountability.

The GDPR has set a global standard for data protection, influencing legislation in countries like Brazil, Japan, and India. However, its implementation has also revealed challenges, such as the difficulty of enforcing rules across global companies and the trade-offs between transparency and intellectual property.

This case demonstrates both the potential and the limitations of regulatory efforts, highlighting the need for continuous refinement and adaptation.

Chapter 6

Corporate Responsibility in AI Development

As Artificial Intelligence (AI) continues to shape industries and influence lives, the role of corporations in its development and deployment has become increasingly significant. Companies are often at the forefront of AI innovation, driving advancements in healthcare, finance, education, and beyond. However, with this power comes responsibility. Corporations must ensure that their AI systems align with ethical principles and contribute positively to society. In this chapter, we explore how businesses can balance profit and purpose, the importance of ethical decision-making, and real-world examples of corporate responsibility in AI.

Why Corporate Responsibility Matters

Corporations play a pivotal role in the AI ecosystem. They control the resources, talent, and infrastructure needed to develop AI systems, and their decisions directly impact how these technologies are used. For example, an AI-powered hiring tool deployed by a major company can influence the career opportunities of thousands of individuals. Similarly, a healthcare AI system used by hospitals can affect the quality of care received by patients.

When corporations prioritize ethical considerations, they can drive meaningful change, setting standards for responsible AI development across industries. Conversely, when profit is prioritized over ethics, the consequences can be severe. From biased algorithms that perpetuate discrimination to data breaches that compromise privacy, the risks of unethical AI practices underscore the need for corporate accountability.

Balancing Profit and Purpose

Businesses face a constant tension between maximizing profits and fulfilling their ethical obligations. In competitive markets, the pressure to innovate quickly and capture market share can lead to shortcuts that compromise ethical standards. For instance, companies may deploy AI systems without thoroughly testing them for bias or reliability, putting users at risk.

However, prioritizing ethics is not just the right thing to do—it is also good for business. Consumers are increasingly demanding transparency and accountability from companies, particularly when it comes to technology. A corporation that demonstrates a commitment to ethical AI practices can build trust and loyalty, enhancing its reputation and long-term success.

Additionally, regulators are holding companies accountable for unethical practices. Laws like the General Data Protection Regulation (GDPR) impose significant penalties for violations, incentivizing businesses to adopt responsible practices. Ethical AI development, therefore, is not just a moral imperative but also a strategic advantage.

Key Elements of Corporate Responsibility in AI

1. Establishing AI Ethics Guidelines

One of the first steps for corporations is to create clear guidelines for ethical AI development. These guidelines should outline the company's commitment to principles such as fairness, transparency, accountability, and privacy. For example, Microsoft's AI Principles emphasize the need for inclusivity, reliability, and trust.

Having a formal set of guidelines provides a framework for decision-making, ensuring that ethical considerations are integrated into every stage of AI development. It also signals to stakeholders—employees, customers, and regulators—that the company takes its responsibilities seriously.

2. Creating Oversight Mechanisms

Accountability requires oversight. Corporations can establish AI ethics boards or review committees to evaluate projects and ensure they align with ethical standards. These boards should include diverse perspectives, bringing together technical experts, ethicists, and representatives from affected communities.

For instance, Google's Advanced Technology External Advisory Council was created to guide the company's use of AI in sensitive areas, such as facial recognition and military applications. While the council faced challenges, its creation highlights the importance of independent oversight in corporate AI governance.

3. Promoting Diversity and Inclusion

AI systems reflect the perspectives of the people who design them. A lack of diversity within development teams can lead to blind spots and biased outcomes. To address this, corporations must prioritize diversity and inclusion at all levels, from hiring practices to leadership roles.

For example, IBM has implemented initiatives to increase diversity in its AI teams, recognizing that a variety of perspectives leads to more robust and fair systems. By fostering an inclusive culture, corporations can reduce the risk of unintended consequences and ensure their AI systems serve a broad range of users.

5. Engaging Stakeholders

Ethical AI development is not just an internal process; it requires engagement with external stakeholders. Corporations should collaborate with governments, academia, and civil society to address complex ethical challenges and develop best practices.

Engaging with stakeholders also includes listening to the concerns of customers and communities affected by AI systems. This feedback can provide valuable insights into potential risks and areas for improvement, helping companies build trust and accountability.

Case Studies: Corporate Responsibility in Action

Case Study 1: Microsoft's AI for Accessibility

Microsoft's AI for Accessibility program demonstrates how corporations can use AI to address societal challenges. The initiative focuses on developing AI tools to empower people with disabilities, such as apps that provide real-time transcription for the hearing impaired. By aligning innovation with social good, Microsoft exemplifies how corporations can integrate ethical principles into their business strategies.

Case Study 2: Facebook's Algorithmic Oversight

In response to criticism over the spread of misinformation on its platform, Facebook created an independent Oversight Board to review content moderation decisions. While the board has faced scrutiny, its creation represents a step toward greater accountability and transparency in the use of AI for content curation.

Case Study 3: IBM's Withdrawal from Facial Recognition

In 2020, IBM announced that it would no longer offer general-purpose facial recognition software, citing concerns about bias and misuse. The company also called for a national dialogue on the use of AI in law enforcement. This decision highlighted IBM's willingness to prioritize ethics over profit, setting an example for other corporations.

The Challenges of Corporate Responsibility

Despite these examples, achieving corporate responsibility in AI is not without challenges. Profit-driven motives can sometimes conflict with ethical goals, particularly in industries where rapid innovation is key to maintaining a competitive edge. Additionally, corporations may face resistance from within, as employees and stakeholders debate the ethical implications of AI projects.

Another challenge is the global nature of AI deployment. A company operating in multiple countries must navigate a patchwork of regulations and cultural norms, making it difficult to maintain consistent ethical standards. For instance, a company might face stricter data protection laws in Europe than in Asia, complicating its approach to privacy.

Chapter 7

The Future of AI Ethics

As Artificial Intelligence (AI) continues to advance at an unprecedented pace, the ethical challenges surrounding its development and deployment are evolving just as rapidly. While current efforts focus on addressing issues such as bias, privacy, and accountability, the future of AI ethics will involve navigating new complexities brought on by emerging technologies, global shifts, and societal transformations. This chapter explores the trends shaping the future of AI ethics, the opportunities they present, and the steps we must take to prepare for an AI-driven world.

Emerging Trends in AI Development

The future of AI will be defined by its increasing sophistication and ubiquity. Emerging trends such as autonomous systems, generative AI, and AI-human collaboration are reshaping how we interact with technology and raising new ethical questions.

1. Autonomous Systems

One significant trend is the rise of **autonomous systems**, such as self-driving cars, delivery drones, and autonomous weapons. These systems operate with minimal human intervention, making decisions in real time based on complex algorithms. While autonomy offers immense potential—such as reducing traffic accidents or improving logistics—it also introduces challenges related to accountability. For instance, if a self-driving car causes an accident, who should be held responsible: the manufacturer, the software developer, or the user? Resolving these questions will require new frameworks for liability and oversight.

2.   Generative AI

Another trend is the rapid growth of **generative AI**, exemplified by tools like ChatGPT and DALL·E. These systems can create realistic text, images, and videos, blurring the line between reality and fiction. While generative AI has creative and commercial applications, it also raises concerns about misinformation, copyright infringement, and the erosion of trust in digital content. Addressing these issues will involve both technical solutions, such as watermarking AI-generated content, and societal efforts to promote digital literacy.

3.   AI-Human Collaboration

Finally, the increasing integration of AI into everyday life is fostering a new era of **AI-human collaboration**. From personal assistants to wearable health monitors, AI is becoming a partner in decision-making rather than just a tool. This shift requires a focus on designing AI systems that are intuitive, transparent, and aligned with human values, ensuring that they enhance rather than undermine our autonomy.

Ethical Opportunities in Emerging AI

While these trends pose challenges, they also present opportunities to rethink and expand our ethical frameworks. For example, the rise of autonomous systems can drive innovation in safety standards, ensuring that all AI systems meet rigorous criteria before deployment. Similarly, generative AI offers a chance to explore new forms of creative expression and collaboration, provided it is developed responsibly.

One of the most exciting opportunities lies in using AI to address global challenges. From climate change to healthcare inequities, AI has the potential to accelerate solutions to some of humanity's most pressing problems. For instance, AI-driven models can predict the impacts of climate change more accurately, helping governments and organizations plan effective mitigation strategies. However, realizing these benefits will require careful attention to ethical considerations, such as ensuring that the use of AI is inclusive and equitable.

Preparing for an AI-Driven World

Preparing for the future of AI ethics involves a proactive approach to addressing emerging challenges and opportunities. This preparation can be broken down into three key areas: education, governance, and collaboration.

1. Building Ethical Awareness through Education

As AI becomes more pervasive, it is essential to educate individuals and organizations about its ethical implications. This includes fostering digital literacy among the general public, equipping people with the skills to critically evaluate AI systems and their impacts. For example, understanding how generative AI works can help individuals identify deepfake content and avoid falling prey to misinformation.

Education must also extend to professionals involved in AI development. Training programs should emphasize the importance of ethical principles, equipping developers, data scientists, and policymakers with the knowledge needed to navigate complex ethical dilemmas. By making ethics a core component of AI education, we can build a workforce that prioritizes responsibility alongside innovation.

2. Strengthening Governance Frameworks

As discussed in earlier chapters, governance is essential for ensuring that AI systems operate responsibly. In the future, governance frameworks must evolve to address the unique challenges posed by emerging technologies. For instance, policies regulating generative AI should account for its potential to disrupt industries, such as journalism and entertainment, while protecting intellectual property rights and promoting fairness.

International collaboration will also play a crucial role in strengthening governance. Given the global nature of AI, countries must work together to establish consistent standards and share best practices. Initiatives like the OECD's Principles on Artificial Intelligence and the UN's work on AI ethics provide a foundation for global cooperation, but more comprehensive efforts will be needed to address the complexities of a rapidly changing technological landscape.

3. Fostering Multidisciplinary Collaboration

AI ethics cannot be addressed in isolation. It requires input from diverse disciplines, including computer science, philosophy, law, sociology, and psychology. Multidisciplinary collaboration ensures that ethical considerations are thoroughly examined from multiple perspectives, leading to more robust and inclusive solutions.

For example, designing an AI system to improve healthcare delivery might involve collaboration between engineers, ethicists, healthcare providers, and patient advocacy groups. Each stakeholder brings unique insights that can help identify risks and opportunities, ensuring that the system aligns with ethical principles and serves the needs of its users.

Collaboration also extends to the broader community. Engaging with affected populations—particularly those who have historically been marginalized—can help uncover blind spots and ensure that AI systems are designed to benefit everyone. This participatory approach not only improves the quality of AI systems but also builds trust and accountability.

Case Study: Ethical Innovation in Climate AI

One promising application of AI is in addressing climate change. Companies like DeepMind have developed AI systems to optimize energy consumption, reduce waste, and accelerate the adoption of renewable energy sources. For instance, DeepMind's AI was used to improve the energy efficiency of Google's data centers, reducing electricity usage by 15%.

However, the use of AI in climate action also raises ethical questions. Who controls the technology, and how are its benefits distributed? If AI-driven solutions disproportionately benefit wealthy countries or corporations, they risk exacerbating global inequalities. To address

33

these concerns, ethical frameworks must ensure that climate AI technologies are accessible, transparent, and inclusive.

Chapter 8

Artificial Intelligence (AI) holds immense promise for addressing some of the most pressing global challenges, from reducing poverty and improving education to combating climate change and enhancing healthcare access. However, the use of AI in global development comes with its own set of ethical considerations. Ensuring that AI serves as a tool for equitable progress requires careful planning, inclusive design, and a commitment to addressing systemic inequalities. This chapter explores the opportunities and challenges of using AI in global development, emphasizing the need for ethical frameworks that prioritize fairness, inclusivity, and sustainability.

The Potential of AI in Global Development

AI's ability to analyze vast amounts of data, identify patterns, and make predictions offers transformative potential for addressing global issues. In healthcare, AI systems can assist in diagnosing diseases, predicting outbreaks, and optimizing resource allocation in underserved regions. For example, AI-driven tools have been used to predict the spread of malaria, enabling governments and organizations to deploy preventive measures more effectively.

In agriculture, AI can help small-scale farmers improve crop yields by providing insights on weather patterns, soil quality, and pest control. Platforms like PlantVillage use AI to identify crop diseases through smartphone photos, empowering farmers with actionable information. Similarly, AI-powered microfinancing platforms are helping underserved communities gain access to credit, fostering economic growth and entrepreneurship.

Education is another area where AI is making an impact. Adaptive learning platforms, powered by AI, personalize educational content to meet the unique needs of each student. This approach is particularly valuable in regions with limited access to quality education, where technology can bridge gaps and provide new opportunities for learning.

Challenges in Deploying AI for Development

While the potential of AI in global development is undeniable, its implementation comes with significant challenges that must be addressed to ensure equitable outcomes.

- **Inequitable Access to AI Technologies**

One of the primary challenges is the unequal distribution of AI resources and infrastructure. While wealthy nations and urban centers benefit from advanced AI systems, rural and low-income regions often lack the necessary technology, internet connectivity, and training to leverage AI effectively. This digital divide risks exacerbating existing inequalities, leaving vulnerable populations further behind.

- **Bias in AI Systems**

Bias in AI systems can have devastating consequences when deployed in global development contexts. For example, AI models trained on data from high-income countries may fail to account for the unique needs and conditions of low-income regions. A healthcare AI system designed to diagnose diseases might underperform in regions where the available data differs significantly from the training dataset, leading to misdiagnoses and unequal outcomes.

- **Privacy and Data Security**

Collecting and processing data in underserved regions raises ethical concerns about privacy and data ownership. In some cases, communities may be unaware of how their data is being used or lack the legal protections to prevent misuse. For instance, AI systems used for public health monitoring must balance the need for data-driven insights with the right to individual privacy.

- **Ethical Oversight and Governance**

The absence of robust governance frameworks in many developing regions can lead to the misuse of AI technologies. For example, AI systems used for surveillance and security may be deployed without adequate safeguards, infringing on civil liberties and enabling authoritarian practices. Establishing ethical oversight mechanisms is critical to preventing harm and ensuring that AI serves the public good.

Principles for Ethical AI in Global Development

To ensure that AI contributes to equitable and sustainable development, its deployment must be guided by ethical principles that prioritize the needs of underserved communities.

- **Inclusivity**

AI systems must be designed to address the unique needs of diverse populations. This includes involving local communities in the design and implementation process to ensure that their voices are heard and their needs are met. For instance, engaging farmers in the development of agricultural AI tools can lead to more relevant and effective solutions.

- **Fairness and Equity**

Fairness requires addressing systemic inequalities in access to AI technologies. Governments, nonprofits, and private companies must collaborate to ensure that AI systems are accessible to all, regardless of socioeconomic status or geographic location. Subsidies, open-source platforms, and community-driven initiatives can help bridge the digital divide.

- Transparency and Accountability

AI systems used in global development must be transparent, with clear explanations of how decisions are made and who is responsible for the outcomes. For example, an AI-powered loan approval system should provide applicants with understandable explanations of why their applications were approved or denied.

4. Sustainability

AI technologies should be developed and deployed with a focus on long-term sustainability. This includes considering the environmental impact of AI systems, such as the energy consumption of data centers, and ensuring that solutions are resilient to changing conditions.

Case Study: AI in Disaster Management

One notable application of AI in global development is its use in disaster management. Following the 2015 Nepal earthquake, AI systems were used to analyze satellite imagery and identify affected areas in real time. This information enabled relief organizations to prioritize resources and reach vulnerable populations more quickly.

However, this success also highlighted challenges. The reliance on satellite data raised questions about data privacy and ownership, as well as the risk of excluding communities not visible in the imagery. This case underscores the need for ethical frameworks that balance technological efficiency with inclusivity and privacy.

The Role of Collaboration

Addressing the challenges of AI in global development requires collaboration across sectors and borders. Governments, international organizations, academia, and the private sector must work together to create inclusive AI solutions that address systemic inequalities. For example, partnerships between tech companies and nonprofits can combine technical expertise with local knowledge, leading to more effective and equitable outcomes.

Collaboration must also extend to affected communities. By involving local stakeholders in the decision-making process, organizations can ensure that AI systems reflect the needs and values of the people they are designed to serve. This participatory approach not only improves the quality of AI solutions but also builds trust and accountability.

As Artificial Intelligence (AI) continues to reshape industries and redefine how we live, preparing for an AI-driven world has become an urgent priority. Whether it's in education, employment, governance, or personal life, AI's influence is profound and far-reaching. To navigate this transformation, individuals, organizations, and societies must cultivate awareness, foster education, and promote public participation in shaping the ethical trajectory of AI. This chapter focuses on actionable steps to prepare for a future where AI plays an increasingly central role.

Building Awareness of AI's Impact

Understanding the opportunities and risks of AI is the first step in preparing for its widespread adoption. Many people encounter AI daily without fully recognizing its presence—whether it's through personalized recommendations on streaming platforms, facial recognition on smartphones, or algorithms that determine loan approvals. This lack of awareness can lead to misplaced trust or unnecessary fear, both of which hinder our ability to engage with AI effectively.

Public education campaigns are essential to demystify AI and explain how it affects individuals and communities. Governments, educational institutions, and media organizations can play a key role in fostering this understanding. For example, documentaries, public workshops, and accessible online resources can help people learn about AI's capabilities and limitations. Awareness also involves addressing misconceptions, such as the belief that AI is inherently neutral or infallible, when in reality, it reflects the biases and values of its creators.

Fostering AI Literacy in Education

Education is one of the most powerful tools for preparing individuals to thrive in an AI-driven world. Schools and universities must adapt their curricula to include AI literacy, ensuring that students understand the basics of how AI works, its applications, and its ethical implications. This knowledge is not just for aspiring data scientists or engineers—it is essential for everyone.

For younger students, AI education can begin with interactive lessons that explain concepts like machine learning and pattern recognition in simple terms. For example, students might experiment with AI tools to see how algorithms classify images or predict outcomes based on data. These activities can spark curiosity and help students see AI as a tool they can shape rather than a force beyond their control.

For older students and professionals, education should delve deeper into the technical, social, and ethical dimensions of AI. Topics like algorithmic bias, data privacy, and the societal impacts of automation should be central to AI literacy programs. Partnerships between tech companies and educational institutions can provide access to cutting-edge tools and real-world case studies, making learning more practical and impactful.

Promoting Public Participation in AI Governance

AI governance should not be the exclusive domain of governments, corporations, and academics. Public participation is crucial to ensure that AI systems align with the values and priorities of the communities they serve. This participation can take many forms, from public consultations and citizen assemblies to online forums and advocacy campaigns.

One example of public participation is the use of **citizens' juries**, where a diverse group of individuals is brought together to deliberate on a specific AI-related issue, such as facial recognition in public spaces or the ethical implications of autonomous weapons. These juries provide valuable insights into public sentiment and help policymakers make informed decisions that reflect societal values.

Another avenue for engagement is community-driven AI projects. For instance, local governments and organizations can involve residents in designing AI systems that address specific challenges, such as traffic management or public health. This participatory approach not only improves the relevance and acceptance of AI solutions but also empowers communities to take an active role in shaping their future.

Preparing for Workforce Transformation

AI is expected to disrupt the labor market significantly, automating repetitive tasks while creating new opportunities in areas such as data analysis, AI development, and cybersecurity. Preparing for this transformation requires a proactive approach to workforce development, with a focus on reskilling and upskilling.

Governments and businesses must invest in training programs that equip workers with the skills needed to succeed in an AI-driven economy. These programs should prioritize not only technical skills, such as coding and data management, but also soft skills like critical thinking, creativity, and emotional intelligence, which are less likely to be automated.

For example, a factory worker whose role is automated by AI might transition into a maintenance position that requires understanding how to operate and troubleshoot AI systems. Similarly, healthcare workers can be trained to use AI tools that enhance diagnostics and patient care, blending human expertise with machine efficiency.

Addressing Ethical Challenges

Preparing for an AI-driven world also means grappling with the ethical challenges that come with its adoption. Issues such as privacy, bias, and accountability will only grow more complex as AI systems become more integrated into daily life. Addressing these challenges requires a collective commitment to ethical principles, backed by robust governance and public accountability.

One way to build ethical awareness is through **AI ethics councils** that include representatives from diverse sectors and communities. These councils can evaluate the ethical implications of proposed AI systems, ensuring that they align with societal values. Public reporting on the council's findings can further promote transparency and trust.

Another critical step is encouraging individuals to advocate for ethical AI. By raising their voices through petitions, campaigns, or direct engagement with policymakers, citizens can hold organizations accountable and push for the responsible use of AI.

Case Study: Finland's AI Literacy Program

Finland offers an inspiring example of how to prepare a society for an AI-driven future. The government launched an online course called "Elements of AI," designed to teach citizens the basics of AI in an accessible and engaging way. The course covers topics such as machine learning, neural networks, and the societal implications of AI, requiring no prior technical knowledge.

The initiative has been a resounding success, with thousands of participants from diverse backgrounds, including students, retirees, and professionals. By empowering its population with AI literacy, Finland has demonstrated the power of education in preparing for technological change.

The Role of Organizations in Preparation

While governments and educational institutions play critical roles, businesses and organizations must also contribute to preparing for an AI-driven world. This includes fostering a culture of continuous learning within their workforce, adopting ethical AI practices, and collaborating with stakeholders to address broader societal challenges.

For instance, tech companies can support AI literacy by providing free resources, hosting workshops, and participating in public education campaigns. Businesses in other sectors can lead by example, showcasing how AI can be used responsibly to enhance operations while respecting ethical principles.

Education is one of the most transformative applications of Artificial Intelligence (AI), with the potential to revolutionize how we teach and learn. From personalized learning experiences to automated administrative tasks, AI can enhance efficiency, accessibility, and inclusivity in education systems worldwide. However, as with any powerful tool, the integration of AI into education raises ethical questions and challenges that must be carefully addressed. This chapter explores how AI is reshaping education, its potential benefits, and the ethical considerations that come with its adoption.

The Potential of AI in Education

AI's role in education extends beyond automating mundane tasks. It has the capacity to create highly personalized learning experiences, adapt to the needs of individual students, and provide educators with actionable insights to improve teaching strategies. These applications are already making an impact in classrooms around the world.

One of AI's most promising contributions is its ability to deliver **personalized learning**. Traditional education often struggles to cater to the diverse needs of students in a single classroom. AI-powered platforms, however, can analyze a student's performance in real time, identify areas where they are struggling, and provide tailored content to address their specific challenges. For example, adaptive learning systems like DreamBox or Khan Academy adjust lesson difficulty based on a student's progress, ensuring that each learner moves at their own pace.

AI also has the potential to break down barriers to education. Language translation tools powered by AI, such as Google Translate, enable students from different linguistic backgrounds to access educational resources in their preferred language. Similarly, AI-driven applications can assist students with disabilities by offering tools like real-time transcription for hearing-impaired learners or text-to-speech systems for those with visual impairments.

Administrative tasks in education can also be streamlined through AI, freeing up educators to focus on teaching. For instance, AI can automate grading for multiple-choice and short-answer questions, saving teachers hours of time. AI systems can also assist in creating lesson plans, scheduling, and even managing parent-teacher communication.

Case Study: Personalized Learning with Duolingo

Duolingo, a popular language-learning platform, exemplifies how AI can enhance personalized education. The app uses AI algorithms to analyze how users interact with lessons, identifying their strengths and weaknesses. Based on this analysis, Duolingo adapts the difficulty and content of future lessons to ensure learners remain engaged and challenged. This approach has made language learning more accessible and effective for millions of users worldwide.

Ethical Considerations in AI-Driven Education

While the benefits of AI in education are compelling, its integration also raises significant ethical concerns. These challenges must be addressed to ensure that AI enhances education equitably and responsibly.

- **Privacy and Data Security**

4. AI systems in education often rely on collecting and analyzing large amounts of data about students, including their academic performance, behavioral patterns, and even personal information. This raises concerns about how that data is stored, who has access to it, and how it might be used. For example, could a student's learning data

inadvertently influence their opportunities for college admission or employment?

To address these concerns, educational institutions must prioritize data security and transparency. Students and parents should have clear information about what data is being collected and how it will be used. Governments and organizations should establish strict regulations to protect student privacy, similar to the General Data Protection Regulation (GDPR) in Europe.

- **Bias in AI Systems**

Bias in AI algorithms can perpetuate inequalities in education. For instance, if an AI system is trained on data that reflects historical disparities in academic performance across demographic groups, it may unfairly disadvantage certain students. This could lead to situations where students from underrepresented communities receive fewer opportunities for advanced learning.

To mitigate bias, developers must ensure that the datasets used to train AI systems are diverse and representative. Regular audits and fairness testing can also help identify and address disparities in how AI systems perform across different student populations.

- **Teacher Autonomy and the Role of Human Educators**

AI's growing role in education raises questions about the balance between technology and human interaction. While AI can provide valuable insights and automation, it cannot replace the empathy, creativity, and nuanced understanding that human educators bring to the classroom. Over-reliance on AI could undermine the role of teachers, reducing their autonomy and diminishing the human element of education.

To avoid this, AI should be viewed as a tool that supports educators rather than replaces them. Training programs should help teachers integrate AI into their teaching practices effectively, empowering them to make informed decisions about how and when to use the technology.

Preparing for AI in Education

The successful integration of AI into education requires a proactive and collaborative approach. Schools, governments, and technology providers must work together to address ethical challenges and ensure that AI serves the best interests of students and educators.

- **Developing Ethical Guidelines**

Educational institutions should establish ethical guidelines for the use of AI in classrooms. These guidelines should address issues like data privacy, bias, and transparency, providing a framework for responsible AI adoption. For example, schools might require AI vendors to demonstrate compliance with data protection laws and conduct regular audits of their systems.

- **Fostering Collaboration**

Collaboration between educators, technologists, and policymakers is essential to create AI systems that align with the needs and values of the education community. For instance, involving teachers in the design of AI tools can help ensure that the technology addresses real-world classroom challenges.

- **Promoting AI Literacy**

As AI becomes more integrated into education, students and educators alike must develop a basic understanding of how the technology works and its potential implications. AI literacy programs can help students critically evaluate the AI systems they interact with, empowering them to use the technology responsibly and effectively.

Case Study: AI-Assisted Learning in India

In rural India, where access to quality education is limited, AI-driven learning platforms like Byju's have played a transformative role. Byju's uses AI to adapt lessons to the individual needs of students, helping them improve their understanding of core subjects. The platform has enabled millions of students in underserved areas to access high-quality educational content, demonstrating AI's potential to bridge educational gaps.

Chapter 11

Artificial Intelligence (AI) is transforming the way people manage their money, offering tools that promise to make financial planning, investing, and budgeting more efficient and accessible. From robo-advisors that help individuals build investment portfolios to AI-driven apps that track spending habits, these innovations are reshaping personal finance. However, while AI offers significant benefits, it also raises ethical concerns about privacy, transparency, and equity. This chapter explores how AI is revolutionizing personal finance, the opportunities it presents, and the ethical considerations it demands.

The Rise of AI in Personal Finance

AI's ability to process vast amounts of data and identify patterns makes it ideally suited for personal finance applications. Traditional financial management often requires expertise, time, and resources that many individuals lack. AI bridges this gap by automating complex processes and providing tailored advice that is accessible to a wider audience.

One of the most popular applications of AI in personal finance is **robo-advisors**. These digital platforms use AI algorithms to provide investment advice based on an individual's financial goals, risk tolerance, and time horizon. For example, platforms like Betterment and Wealthfront automatically rebalance portfolios and optimize investments, making sophisticated financial strategies available to people who may not have access to traditional financial advisors.

AI is also revolutionizing **budgeting and expense tracking**. Apps like Mint and YNAB (You Need A Budget) analyze users' spending patterns, categorize expenses, and offer personalized suggestions to help them save money. By providing real-time insights, these tools empower individuals to make informed financial decisions.

Additionally, AI plays a crucial role in **credit scoring and lending**. Lenders use AI algorithms to assess creditworthiness, analyzing factors like income, spending habits, and credit history. This approach allows for faster and more accurate loan decisions, expanding access to credit for individuals who might have been overlooked by traditional methods.

Benefits of AI in Personal Finance

AI-driven tools offer several advantages that can help individuals take control of their financial well-being:

1. **Accessibility**: AI democratizes financial management by providing affordable and user-friendly tools. Even those with limited financial literacy can benefit from personalized advice and automated processes.

2. **Efficiency**: Tasks like tracking expenses, managing investments, and applying for loans are streamlined through AI, saving time and effort.

3. **Personalization**: AI systems tailor financial advice to individual needs, making recommendations based on unique circumstances and goals.

4. **Fraud Detection**: AI-powered systems are highly effective at identifying unusual activity in financial accounts, helping users detect and prevent fraud quickly.

Case Study: Chatbots in Banking

AI chatbots like Erica by Bank of America and Eno by Capital One have become integral to modern banking. These chatbots provide real-time assistance to customers, answering queries, tracking expenses, and even offering tips to improve financial health. For example, Erica can analyze spending habits and suggest ways to save money, while Eno alerts users to unusual charges on their accounts. These tools enhance customer experience by combining convenience with proactive financial advice.

Ethical Challenges in AI-Driven Finance

While AI has the potential to improve personal finance, it also introduces ethical concerns that must be addressed to ensure fairness and trust.

o **Privacy and Data Security**

AI-driven financial tools rely heavily on personal data, including transaction histories, income details, and spending habits. While this data is necessary for providing personalized advice, it also poses risks. A data breach or misuse of information could have severe consequences for individuals' financial security.

To mitigate these risks, companies must adopt robust data protection measures and be transparent about how they collect, store, and use personal information. Users should have control over their data, including the ability to opt out of data collection or request its deletion.

o **Transparency in Decision-Making**

AI algorithms used in credit scoring or lending decisions can lack transparency, making it difficult for individuals to understand why they were approved or denied for a loan. This lack of explainability can lead to frustration and erode trust in financial institutions.

Financial organizations must prioritize explainable AI, ensuring that their algorithms can provide clear and understandable reasons for their decisions. For example, if an AI system denies a loan application, it should specify whether the decision was based on income, credit history, or another factor.

o   Bias and Discrimination

AI systems are not immune to bias, particularly if they are trained on historical data that reflects systemic inequalities. For instance, an AI-powered lending system might inadvertently favor applicants from wealthier neighborhoods while disadvantaging those from underprivileged areas.

Addressing bias requires a proactive approach to data selection and algorithm design. Regular audits and fairness testing can help identify and correct disparities, ensuring that AI systems promote equitable outcomes.

o   Over-Reliance on Technology

As AI becomes more integral to personal finance, there is a risk of over-reliance on technology. Individuals may trust AI tools without fully understanding their limitations, potentially leading to poor financial decisions.

Financial literacy initiatives are essential to empower users to critically evaluate the advice provided by AI tools. Education can help individuals balance the benefits of AI with their own judgment and understanding.

Preparing for AI in Personal Finance

To maximize the benefits of AI in personal finance while minimizing its risks, individuals and organizations must adopt a thoughtful and proactive approach.

1.Empowering Users with Financial Literacy

AI tools are most effective when users understand their capabilities and limitations. Financial literacy programs should include lessons on how to use AI-driven tools responsibly, interpret their recommendations, and safeguard personal data.

2. Establishing Ethical Standards

Financial institutions must adopt ethical guidelines for AI use, addressing issues like privacy, bias, and transparency. Regulatory bodies should enforce these standards to ensure accountability and protect consumers.

3. Encouraging Collaboration

Collaboration between financial institutions, technology companies, and regulators can foster innovation while addressing ethical concerns. For example, partnerships between banks and AI developers can lead to more secure and transparent systems.

Case Study: Robo-Advisors and Accessibility

Robo-advisors like Acorns and Stash have democratized investing by lowering barriers to entry. These platforms allow users to start investing with as little as a few dollars, automatically allocating funds based on their financial goals and risk tolerance. By making investing accessible to a wider audience, robo-advisors exemplify how AI can promote financial inclusion.

Artificial Intelligence (AI) is revolutionizing healthcare, offering innovative solutions to improve patient outcomes, streamline administrative tasks, and advance medical research. From diagnosing diseases to predicting outbreaks, AI has the potential to transform how we deliver and receive care. However, the integration of AI in healthcare also raises ethical challenges related to privacy, equity, and accountability. This chapter explores how AI is reshaping the healthcare industry, the opportunities it presents, and the ethical considerations that must guide its adoption.

The Potential of AI in Healthcare

AI's ability to analyze vast amounts of data and identify patterns is particularly valuable in healthcare. Medical professionals often face information overload, with more data than they can reasonably process. AI bridges this gap by quickly analyzing complex datasets, generating insights that support clinical decision-making.

- **Early Disease Detection and Diagnosis**

AI is increasingly used to identify diseases at early stages, when treatment is most effective. For example, AI algorithms can analyze medical images, such as X-rays and MRIs, to detect conditions like cancer, cardiovascular disease, and neurological disorders. In some cases, these systems have demonstrated diagnostic accuracy comparable to, or even surpassing, that of human doctors. Tools like Google's DeepMind have shown promise in diagnosing eye diseases and predicting kidney failure.

- **Personalized Treatment Plans**

AI enables personalized medicine by analyzing a patient's genetic, environmental, and lifestyle factors to recommend tailored treatments. For instance, IBM Watson Health uses AI to assist oncologists in identifying the most effective cancer therapies based on individual patient profiles.

- **Drug Discovery and Development**

AI accelerates the drug discovery process by analyzing biological data to identify potential drug candidates. Traditional drug development can take over a decade and cost billions of dollars, but AI-driven platforms like Insilico Medicine and Atomwise significantly shorten this timeline, reducing costs and bringing life-saving treatments to market faster.

- **Administrative Efficiency**

AI also streamlines administrative tasks, such as scheduling, billing, and documentation. Virtual assistants can transcribe and organize doctors' notes, while AI-powered systems manage appointment bookings and patient follow-ups. By automating these processes, healthcare providers can focus more on patient care.

Case Study: AI in Radiology

One notable application of AI is in radiology, where algorithms analyze medical images to identify abnormalities. A 2020 study demonstrated that an AI system developed by Google outperformed radiologists in detecting breast cancer in mammograms. By reducing false positives and false negatives, the system has the potential to improve early detection and save lives.

Ethical Challenges in AI-Driven Healthcare

While the benefits of AI in healthcare are compelling, its integration raises complex ethical issues that must be addressed to ensure that the technology serves patients equitably and responsibly.

- **Privacy and Data Security**

Healthcare data is highly sensitive, and AI systems often rely on large datasets containing personal information. Ensuring the privacy and security of this data is a critical concern. A data breach or unauthorized use of patient records could have severe consequences, including identity theft and loss of trust in healthcare institutions.

Healthcare organizations must adopt robust encryption, data anonymization, and access controls to protect patient information. Additionally, patients should have transparency and control over how their data is collected, stored, and used.

- **Bias and Inequity**

Bias in AI systems can perpetuate health disparities. For instance, if an AI model is trained on data from predominantly urban or affluent populations, it may not perform as well for patients in rural or underserved areas. Similarly, racial and gender biases in training data can result in unequal treatment recommendations or diagnostic accuracy.

To address these issues, developers must ensure that datasets are diverse and representative. Regular audits and fairness testing can help identify and mitigate biases, promoting equitable outcomes for all patients.

- **Accountability and Liability**

Determining accountability is a key challenge in AI-driven healthcare. If an AI system makes an incorrect diagnosis or treatment recommendation, who is responsible—the developer, the healthcare provider, or the institution that deployed the technology? Clear guidelines and regulatory frameworks are needed to address liability and ensure accountability.

- **Over-Reliance on AI**

While AI can support medical professionals, over-reliance on the technology may undermine clinical judgment. Healthcare providers must maintain their expertise and critical thinking skills, using AI as a tool rather than a replacement for their decision-making capabilities.

Preparing for Ethical AI in Healthcare

To maximize the benefits of AI while minimizing its risks, the healthcare industry must adopt ethical practices that prioritize patient well-being and equity.

- **Developing Ethical Guidelines**

Healthcare institutions should establish clear guidelines for the use of AI, addressing issues like data privacy, bias, and accountability. For example, the World Health Organization (WHO) has published ethical principles for AI in healthcare, emphasizing transparency, inclusivity, and human oversight.

- **Engaging Stakeholders**

Patients, healthcare providers, technologists, and policymakers must collaborate to ensure that AI systems align with societal values and priorities. For instance, involving patient advocacy groups in the design of AI tools can help address concerns and build trust.

- **Promoting AI Literacy in Healthcare**

Healthcare professionals need training to understand how AI works, its limitations, and how to interpret its outputs. AI literacy programs can empower providers to use the technology effectively while maintaining accountability for patient care.

Case Study: AI in Predictive Analytics

AI-powered predictive analytics have been used to identify patients at risk of developing chronic conditions, such as diabetes or heart disease. By analyzing patterns in electronic health records, these systems provide healthcare providers with actionable insights to implement preventive measures. For example, a hospital in California used AI to identify high-risk patients, reducing readmissions and improving outcomes.

The Future of AI in Healthcare

The integration of AI in healthcare is still in its early stages, but its potential is immense. As the technology advances, we can expect to see even more sophisticated applications, such as AI-powered robotic surgeries, real-time health monitoring, and predictive models for pandemic management. However, realizing this potential requires a commitment to ethical principles that prioritize patient safety, equity, and trust.

In the next chapter, we will explore how AI intersects with ethics at a broader societal level, examining its role in shaping governance, human rights, and the future of democracy. Let's continue to uncover the complexities of AI's impact on our world.

Chapter 13

Ethical AI and Society

Artificial Intelligence (AI) is not just a technological innovation; it is a societal force shaping how we live, work, and govern. From influencing public policy to reshaping democratic processes, AI's impact extends far beyond individual applications. As its integration into society deepens, questions of fairness, accountability, and human rights take center stage. In this chapter, we explore how AI is influencing societal structures, the ethical challenges it poses, and the principles required to ensure its responsible use.

AI's Role in Governance and Public Policy

Governments around the world are leveraging AI to improve decision-making, optimize public services, and address complex challenges. For example, AI algorithms analyze data to predict traffic patterns, allocate healthcare resources, and assess the impacts of climate change. These applications promise efficiency and accuracy, but they also raise questions about transparency and accountability.

AI's influence on public policy is particularly evident in **predictive analytics**, where algorithms forecast social outcomes to inform decisions. For instance, predictive policing systems analyze historical crime data to allocate law enforcement resources. While these systems can enhance efficiency, they often perpetuate biases embedded in the data, disproportionately targeting marginalized communities. Addressing these biases requires not only technical solutions but also a commitment to ethical governance that prioritizes fairness and inclusivity.

The Impact of AI on Democracy

AI's role in shaping public discourse and democratic processes is both transformative and fraught with challenges. Social media platforms, powered by AI algorithms, influence what content users see, shaping opinions and behaviors. While this personalization can enhance user experiences, it also creates echo chambers, polarizing societies and undermining democratic debate.

A more concerning issue is the use of AI in **political manipulation**. Deepfake technology, which generates highly realistic but false audio and video, has been used to spread misinformation and disrupt elections. Similarly, bots powered by AI can amplify propaganda, drowning out genuine voices and distorting public opinion.

These developments highlight the need for regulatory frameworks that address the ethical implications of AI in democratic processes. Governments, tech companies, and civil society must work together to promote transparency, combat misinformation, and ensure that AI serves as a tool for democratic empowerment rather than manipulation.

AI and Human Rights

The deployment of AI has significant implications for human rights, particularly in areas like privacy, freedom of expression, and non-discrimination. For example, surveillance systems powered by facial recognition technology have been used to monitor citizens, raising concerns about privacy violations and state overreach.

In some cases, AI systems have been used to restrict freedoms, such as censoring content or tracking political dissent. These practices not only undermine individual rights but also erode trust in technology. Ensuring that AI aligns with human rights requires a global commitment to ethical principles, supported by laws and regulations that protect individual freedoms.

One emerging framework is the **UNESCO Recommendation on the Ethics of Artificial Intelligence**, which emphasizes the importance of human dignity, sustainability, and accountability. Such initiatives provide a foundation for aligning AI development with universal human rights.

Ethical Challenges in Societal AI

Bias and Inequality

AI systems often reflect the biases present in the data they are trained on, leading to unequal outcomes. For instance, algorithms used in hiring or lending decisions may favor certain demographic groups while disadvantaging others. Addressing this issue requires rigorous fairness testing and a commitment to inclusivity in AI design.

Accountability and Transparency

When AI systems influence societal decisions, transparency becomes critical. Citizens have a right to understand how decisions are made, particularly in areas like criminal justice or public resource allocation. Ensuring accountability requires mechanisms for oversight, including audits and public reporting.

Power Imbalances

The deployment of AI often concentrates power in the hands of governments and corporations, leaving individuals with limited control over how technology affects their lives. Empowering citizens through education, advocacy, and participatory governance is essential to address these imbalances.

Case Study: AI in Citizen Engagement

In Taiwan, the government has used AI-powered platforms to enhance citizen participation in policymaking. The platform, known as vTaiwan, allows citizens to discuss and deliberate on proposed policies, using AI to analyze and summarize public input. This approach demonstrates how AI can be used to strengthen democratic processes and foster trust between governments and citizens.

Building an Ethical Framework for Societal AI

Ensuring that AI serves society equitably and responsibly requires a robust ethical framework built on the following principles:

- **Inclusivity**

AI systems must be designed to reflect the diversity of the populations they serve. This includes involving marginalized communities in the design and implementation process to ensure their needs and perspectives are represented.

- **Transparency**

Decisions influenced by AI should be explainable and accessible to the public. For example, an AI system used in public housing allocation should provide clear reasons for its recommendations, allowing citizens to understand and challenge decisions if necessary.

- **Accountability**

Governments and organizations must be held accountable for the societal impacts of AI systems. This includes establishing clear guidelines for responsibility and creating mechanisms for redress when harm occurs.

- **Collaboration**

The ethical challenges of societal AI cannot be addressed in isolation. Multistakeholder collaboration—between governments, corporations, academia, and civil society—is essential for creating comprehensive and effective solutions.

Chapter 14

AI and Sustainability

Artificial Intelligence (AI) holds immense potential to address some of the most pressing environmental challenges, from climate change mitigation to resource conservation. By analyzing data, optimizing processes, and predicting outcomes, AI can accelerate efforts toward a more sustainable future. However, AI also has an environmental footprint, particularly in terms of energy consumption and resource use. This chapter explores how AI can contribute to sustainability, the challenges it presents, and the ethical considerations necessary to balance innovation with ecological responsibility.

AI's Role in Addressing Environmental Challenges

AI's ability to process vast amounts of data and generate actionable insights makes it a powerful tool for tackling complex environmental issues. Its applications span a wide range of areas, including climate modeling, renewable energy optimization, and wildlife conservation.

Climate Change Mitigation

AI is playing a key role in understanding and combating climate change. Advanced models use AI to analyze historical climate data and predict future trends, enabling governments and organizations to plan more effectively. For example, AI systems have been used to predict extreme weather events, helping communities prepare for hurricanes, floods, and droughts.

AI also supports carbon reduction efforts by optimizing energy usage. Smart grids powered by AI can predict electricity demand, allocate resources efficiently, and integrate renewable energy sources like wind and solar. Google, for instance, has used AI to reduce the energy consumption of its data centers by up to 40%, showcasing the technology's potential to improve energy efficiency on a large scale.

Wildlife Conservation and Biodiversity

AI-powered tools are being used to monitor wildlife populations and protect endangered species. Drones equipped with AI algorithms can analyze habitats, track animal movements, and identify threats like poaching or habitat destruction. In Africa, AI-driven cameras have been deployed to detect and alert rangers to illegal poaching activities, helping preserve biodiversity.

Sustainable Agriculture

AI can enhance agricultural sustainability by optimizing crop yields, reducing water usage, and minimizing chemical inputs. Tools like FarmLogs and John Deere's AI-driven equipment analyze soil health, weather conditions, and crop performance, providing farmers with data-driven recommendations for sustainable practices.

Case Study: AI for Renewable Energy

One of the most promising applications of AI in sustainability is its role in optimizing renewable energy systems. DeepMind, a subsidiary of Alphabet, developed an AI model to predict the energy output of wind farms 36 hours in advance. This predictive capability allows grid operators to better integrate wind power into energy systems, reducing reliance on fossil fuels and enhancing the stability of renewable energy networks.

The Environmental Costs of AI

While AI can drive sustainability efforts, it is not without its own environmental impact. Training large AI models requires significant computational resources, resulting in high energy consumption and carbon emissions. For example, training a single deep learning model can generate as much carbon dioxide as five cars over their lifetime.

Additionally, the production and disposal of hardware used in AI systems contribute to electronic waste, a growing environmental concern. The mining of rare earth elements needed for processors and other components often leads to habitat destruction and pollution, further compounding AI's ecological footprint.

To address these issues, researchers and developers must adopt strategies to reduce AI's environmental impact. This includes using more energy-efficient algorithms, leveraging renewable energy sources for data centers, and recycling electronic components responsibly.

Ethical Considerations in AI and Sustainability

Balancing the benefits of AI for sustainability with its environmental costs requires a commitment to ethical principles that prioritize long-term ecological health.

Energy Efficiency

Developers must prioritize energy-efficient AI models and algorithms, minimizing the carbon footprint of training and deploying these systems. Organizations like OpenAI and NVIDIA are exploring techniques to optimize computational efficiency, making AI systems more sustainable.

Transparency in Environmental Impact

Companies and institutions using AI should disclose the environmental costs associated with their systems. For example, providing data on the energy consumption of AI models can encourage accountability and promote the adoption of greener practices.

Equitable Access to AI Solutions

AI-driven sustainability efforts should benefit all communities, including those most vulnerable to environmental challenges. This requires designing solutions that are accessible and affordable for low-income and rural populations, ensuring that AI contributes to global environmental equity.

Collaborative Innovation

Addressing environmental challenges is a global effort, requiring collaboration between governments, corporations, academia, and civil society. Partnerships can accelerate the development and deployment of AI solutions that prioritize sustainability, combining technical expertise with local knowledge.

Case Study: AI in Circular Economy

AI is driving the transition to a circular economy, where resources are reused and recycled rather than discarded. For example, AI-powered systems are used in waste management to sort recyclables more efficiently, reducing landfill contributions. Companies like TOMRA Sorting Solutions leverage AI to identify and separate materials, optimizing recycling processes and conserving resources.

Preparing for a Sustainable AI Future

To ensure that AI serves as a force for sustainability, we must adopt practices that align technological innovation with ecological responsibility.

- **Developing Green AI Standards**

Governments and organizations should establish standards for "Green AI," emphasizing energy efficiency and sustainability in AI development. These standards can guide researchers and companies in designing systems that minimize environmental impact.

- **Educating Stakeholders**

Raising awareness about the environmental costs and benefits of AI is essential. Educational programs can help developers, policymakers, and the public understand the trade-offs involved and encourage sustainable practices.

- **Promoting Policy and Regulation**

Policymakers must implement regulations that incentivize sustainable AI practices, such as tax credits for energy-efficient technologies or penalties for excessive energy consumption. International agreements can further align efforts to address the global environmental impact of AI.

Chapter 15

AI in Creative Industries

Artificial Intelligence (AI) is revolutionizing creative fields, from art and music to literature and film. By generating new ideas, enhancing workflows, and democratizing access to creative tools, AI is reshaping how we create and experience culture. However, as AI takes on a greater role in creativity, it also raises questions about authorship, originality, and ethical responsibility. This chapter explores how AI is transforming the creative industries, the opportunities it offers, and the challenges it presents.

AI's Impact on Creativity

Traditionally, creativity has been seen as a uniquely human trait—an expression of individuality and imagination. However, AI's ability to analyze vast datasets, identify patterns, and generate content is challenging this notion. Today, AI tools are assisting artists, writers, and musicians in creating works that were once thought to be beyond the reach of machines.

Generative Art and Design

AI algorithms like DALL·E and DeepArt use machine learning to create stunning visual artworks. These systems analyze existing art styles and generate original pieces that mimic human creativity. Architects and designers are also using AI to explore new possibilities in form and function, creating structures that are both innovative and sustainable.

Music Composition and Production

AI-driven platforms like AIVA (Artificial Intelligence Virtual Artist) compose music in various styles, from classical to electronic. These tools are being used by musicians to generate melodies, harmonies, and even entire compositions. AI is also enhancing music production by automating tasks like mixing, mastering, and sound design.

Writing and Storytelling

AI is increasingly used in writing, from generating news articles to assisting authors with creative writing. Tools like ChatGPT and Sudowrite can draft prose, suggest plot twists, or refine dialogue, making the writing process faster and more collaborative. AI is even being used in filmmaking, where algorithms analyze audience preferences to suggest storylines or optimize scripts.

Game Development

AI is transforming the gaming industry by creating more immersive and dynamic experiences. Procedural generation algorithms design game worlds, while AI-powered non-player characters (NPCs) adapt to player behavior, making games feel more responsive and engaging.

Case Study: AI and Generative Music

AIVA, one of the leading AI tools for music composition, is used to create original scores for films, video games, and advertisements. By analyzing thousands of compositions from renowned composers, AIVA generates pieces that are stylistically similar but entirely original. This tool is particularly valuable for creators with limited resources, democratizing access to high-quality music production.

Opportunities in AI-Driven Creativity

AI is not only enhancing creativity but also making it more accessible. By automating repetitive tasks and lowering barriers to entry, AI allows more people to participate in creative processes.

Democratizing Creativity

AI tools enable individuals without formal training to create professional-quality work. For instance, platforms like Canva, powered by AI, allow users to design graphics and presentations with ease. Similarly, tools like Jasper AI assist non-writers in producing compelling content.

Enhancing Collaboration

AI fosters collaboration between humans and machines, opening new possibilities for co-creation. For example, an artist might use AI to generate a rough sketch, which they then refine manually. This synergy between human intuition and machine precision can lead to innovative outcomes.

Expanding Possibilities

AI can push the boundaries of what is creatively possible, exploring ideas and styles that humans might not conceive on their own. For instance, AI-generated artworks often combine elements from disparate styles or eras, resulting in unique and unexpected creations.

Ethical Challenges in AI Creativity

As AI becomes a more prominent force in creative industries, it raises significant ethical questions that must be addressed to ensure fairness, originality, and accountability.

- **Authorship and Ownership**

Who owns the rights to an AI-generated work? This question has sparked debates across creative industries. For example, if an AI composes a song, does the ownership belong to the developer of the AI, the user who generated the piece, or neither? Clear guidelines are needed to address these issues and protect the rights of creators.

- **Originality and Plagiarism**

AI systems often learn from existing works, raising concerns about originality and copyright infringement. For instance, an AI-generated painting might closely resemble a copyrighted piece, leading to disputes over intellectual property. Ensuring that AI-generated content is truly original requires careful design and oversight.

- **Cultural Appropriation and Bias**

AI tools trained on culturally specific datasets might unintentionally replicate or misappropriate cultural elements. For example, an AI that generates music inspired by indigenous traditions must be used responsibly to respect the cultural heritage it draws from.

- **Impact on Human Creators**

While AI democratizes access to creative tools, it also poses challenges for professional artists, writers, and musicians. The availability of AI-generated content might devalue human creativity, making it harder for traditional creators to compete. Supporting human creators in the age of AI requires fostering a culture that values originality, craftsmanship, and authenticity.

Case Study: Deepfake Art and Ethics

Deepfake technology, which uses AI to generate realistic but fabricated videos and images, has sparked both admiration and controversy. While deepfakes have been used creatively in films and art installations, they have also raised ethical concerns about misinformation and identity theft. For instance, deepfakes of public figures have been used to spread false narratives, highlighting the need for regulation and transparency in the use of this technology.

Guiding Principles for AI in Creativity

To ensure that AI enhances rather than undermines creative industries, its use must be guided by ethical principles:

- **Transparency**

Creators and consumers should be aware when AI is involved in generating content. For example, labeling AI-generated artworks or music can help audiences make informed judgments about the originality and authenticity of a piece.

- **Respect for Intellectual Property**

AI developers and users must respect existing copyrights and ensure that their systems do not infringe on the rights of human creators. This includes implementing safeguards to prevent plagiarism and appropriation.

- **Empowering Human Creativity**

AI should be seen as a tool that enhances human creativity, not a replacement for it. Policies and practices that support human creators, such as fair compensation and access to training, are essential for maintaining a vibrant creative ecosystem.

- **Inclusivity and Cultural Sensitivity**

AI systems should be designed and used in ways that respect diverse cultural traditions and avoid perpetuating stereotypes or biases. Engaging with communities and stakeholders during the development process can help achieve this goal.

Reference List

1. **Books and Publications**
   o Bostrom, N. (2014). *Superintelligence: Paths, Dangers, Strategies*. Oxford University Press.
   o Russell, S., & Norvig, P. (2020). *Artificial Intelligence: A Modern Approach*. Pearson.
   o O'Neil, C. (2016). *Weapons of Math Destruction: How Big Data Increases Inequality and Threatens Democracy*. Crown Publishing Group.
   o Tegmark, M. (2017). *Life 3.0: Being Human in the Age of Artificial Intelligence*. Vintage.
2. **Reports and Guidelines**
   o European Union. (2021). *Proposal for a Regulation Laying Down Harmonized Rules on Artificial Intelligence (Artificial Intelligence Act)*.
   o UNESCO. (2021). *Recommendation on the Ethics of Artificial Intelligence*.
   o IEEE Global Initiative on Ethics of Autonomous and Intelligent Systems. (2019). *Ethically Aligned Design, First Edition*.
   o OECD. (2019). *OECD Principles on Artificial Intelligence*.
3. **Academic Articles**
   o Mittelstadt, B. D., Allo, P., Taddeo, M., Wachter, S., & Floridi, L. (2016). *The Ethics of Algorithms: Mapping the Debate*. Big Data & Society.
   o Floridi, L., & Cowls, J. (2019). *A Unified Framework of Five Principles for AI in Society*. Harvard Data Science Review.

4. **Case Studies**
    o *IBM Watson in Healthcare*: Use of AI in oncology for tailored treatment suggestions (IBM, 2017).
    o *COMPAS Algorithm Bias*: ProPublica's investigation into bias in criminal justice predictive algorithms (ProPublica, 2016).
5. **Media and Articles**
    o Knight, W. (2017). *The Dark Secret at the Heart of AI*. MIT Technology Review.
    o Crawford, K., & Joler, V. (2018). *Anatomy of an AI System*. AI Now Institute.
    o Harari, Y. N. (2018). *Why Technology Favors Tyranny*. The Atlantic.
6. **Web Resources**
    o DeepMind. (2020). *AI for Social Good*. Retrieved from www.deepmind.com
    o OpenAI. (2021). *GPT and Generative Models Overview*. Retrieved from www.openai.com
7. **Tools and Frameworks**
    o IBM AI Fairness 360: A toolkit for detecting and mitigating bias in machine learning models.
    o Google What-If Tool: An interactive platform for testing AI fairness and transparency.

Appendix A: Glossary of Terms

- **Artificial Intelligence (AI):** The simulation of human intelligence by machines, enabling them to perform tasks like learning, reasoning, and decision-making.
- **Bias:** A systemic and often unintended prejudice in AI decision-making caused by flawed data or design.
- **Deep Learning:** A subset of machine learning that uses neural networks with many layers to analyze and interpret complex data.
- **Ethical AI:** The practice of developing AI systems that align with principles of fairness, accountability, transparency, and inclusivity.
- **Generative AI:** AI systems that create new content, such as images, text, or music, based on learned patterns from existing data.
- **Machine Learning (ML):** A method of teaching computers to learn and make predictions from data without explicit programming for every scenario.
- **Transparency:** The practice of making AI systems understandable and explainable to users and stakeholders.

Appendix B: Resources for Ethical AI Development

This section lists tools and frameworks designed to help developers and organizations adopt ethical AI practices.

1. **AI Fairness 360 (IBM):** An open-source toolkit for identifying and mitigating bias in AI systems.

   o Website: aif360.mybluemix.net

2. **Google's What-If Tool:** A visualization tool for exploring AI model behavior and detecting potential bias.

   o Website: pair-code.github.io/what-if-tool

3. **Pytorch and TensorFlow Ethics Modules:** Add-ons to popular machine learning frameworks to incorporate fairness and transparency into AI models.

4. **The AI Ethics Guidelines Global Inventory:** A comprehensive database of ethical AI guidelines worldwide.

   o Website: algorithmwatch.org

Appendix C: Case Studies

Detailed discussions of significant AI applications and their ethical implications.

1. **COMPAS and Algorithmic Bias in Criminal Justice**

   o **Summary:** COMPAS, a tool used to predict recidivism, was found to disproportionately label Black defendants as high risk compared to white defendants.
   o **Key Lessons:** Highlights the importance of fairness testing and the need for diverse, representative training datasets.
2. **Google DeepMind's Energy Efficiency Efforts**

   o **Summary:** Google used DeepMind's AI to optimize its data center cooling systems, reducing energy consumption by 40%.
   o **Key Lessons:** Demonstrates how AI can contribute to sustainability when paired with responsible practices.
3. **Facial Recognition Technology and Privacy**

   o **Summary:** The use of facial recognition in public surveillance raises privacy and human rights concerns, especially in authoritarian regimes.
   o **Key Lessons:** Emphasizes the importance of balancing security with individual freedoms.

Appendix D: Ethical AI Frameworks and Guidelines

This section provides references to widely recognized ethical AI frameworks and guidelines.

1. **EU's Ethics Guidelines for Trustworthy AI**

   o Principles: Fairness, transparency, accountability, and human oversight.
   o Website: ec.europa.eu/digital-strategy

2. **UNESCO's AI Ethics Recommendations**

   o Focus: Promoting human dignity, sustainability, and inclusivity.
   o Website: unesco.org

3. **IEEE's Ethically Aligned Design**

   o Overview: A detailed framework for aligning AI systems with ethical and societal values.
   o Website: standards.ieee.org

Appendix E: Further Reading

Books, articles, and academic papers for readers interested in exploring AI ethics further.

1. **Books**
   - *Superintelligence: Paths, Dangers, Strategies* by Nick Bostrom
   - *Weapons of Math Destruction* by Cathy O'Neil
   - *The Big Nine* by Amy Webb

2. **Articles**
   - "The Ethical Implications of AI Bias" (*MIT Technology Review*)
   - "How to Make AI Fair" (*Nature*)

3. **Academic Papers**
   - "On the Fairness of Machine Learning Models" (*Journal of Artificial Intelligence Research*)
   - "Ethical Guidelines for AI Development" (*Proceedings of the AAAI Conference on Artificial Intelligence*)

Appendix F: Tools for Exploring AI

Practical tools for readers to experiment with AI and better understand its capabilities.

1. **Runway ML:** A platform for creating generative art, videos, and other creative projects using AI.

    o Website: runwayml.com
2. **Hugging Face:** A library for building and experimenting with natural language processing (NLP) models.

    o Website: huggingface.co
3. **Teachable Machine:** A Google project that allows users to create AI models without coding.

    o Website: teachablemachine.withgoogle.com